Mami

For my dad, Joe, who I didn't get a chance to know. —J.C-L.

For my parents, Manny & Sony. —K.S.

Pronunciation Guide

lumpia: loom-pya

Ma Mon Luk: mah mohn louk

mee/mi: me

Ng Shih: ung suh

pingga: ping-ga

siomai: shoh-my

siopao: shoh-pow

Text copyright © 2024 by Jacqueline Chio-Lauri
Illustrations copyright © 2024 by Kristin Sorra

Millbrook Press™
An imprint of Lerner Publishing Group, Inc.
241 First Avenue North
Minneapolis, MN 55401 USA

For reading levels and more information, look up this title at www.lernerbooks.com.

Photos courtesy of: Kristin Sorra (family photo); Judge Florentino Floro/Wikimedia Commons PD (restaurant, Ma Mon Luk portrait and soup).

Designed by Viet Chu.
Main body text set in Plantin Std. Typeface provided by Monotype Typography.
The illustrations in this book were created digitally.

Library of Congress Cataloging-in-Publication Data

Names: Chio-Lauri, Jacqueline, author. | Sorra, Kristin, illustrator.
Title: Mami King : how Ma Mon Luk found love, riches, and the perfect bowl of soup / Jacqueline Chio-Lauri ; illustrated by Kristin Sorra.
Description: Minneapolis : Millbrook Press, [2024] | Includes bibliographical references. | Audience: Ages 7–11 | Audience: Grades 2–3 | Summary: "The true story of an intrepid young man, Ma Mon Luk, who leaves China for the Philippines, desperate to earn a living—and the approval of the parents of the woman he loves" —Provided by publisher.
Identifiers: LCCN 2023021734 (print) | LCCN 2023021735 (ebook) | ISBN 9781728492353 (lib. bdg.) | ISBN 9798765619148 (epub)
Subjects: LCSH: Luk, Ma Mon, 1896–1961—Juvenile literature. | Restaurateurs—Philippines—Biography—Juvenile literature. | Cooking, Chinese—Juvenile literature. | Noodle soups—Philippines—Juvenile literature. | BISAC: JUVENILE NONFICTION / Cooking & Food
Classification: LCC TX910.5.L84 C45 2024 (print) | LCC TX910.5.L84 (ebook) | DDC 647.95092 [B]—dc23/eng/20230711

LC record available at https://lccn.loc.gov/2023021734
LC ebook record available at https://lccn.loc.gov/2023021735

Manufactured in the United States of America
1-53231-51208-11/16/2023

Mami King

How MA MON LUK found LOVE, RICHES, and the PERFECT BOWL of SOUP

Written by **Jacqueline Chio-Lauri**

Illustrated by **Kristin Sorra**

M Millbrook Press / Minneapolis

A steamship pulled Ma Mon Luk away from the bustling port and Ng Shih, the girl he loved.

The words of Ng Shih's rich parents echoed in his ears like the slapping of waves against the ship's hull:

"No daughter of ours is marrying a poor man like you!"

I'll show them! Ma vowed.

Aboard, the painful truth of the words
of Ng Shih's parents was plain to see.

The rich and the poor, like
oil and water, didn't mix.

Ma arrived in the Philippines ready to make a new start. Day after day, he wandered the streets of Manila's Chinatown in search of a way to earn a living.

A wayside cook who spoke Ma's native tongue swirled noodles in a vast iron wok.

A peddler balanced a tray of food on her head and called, "Lumpia for sale!"

A street vendor lifted a bamboo basket from a stack, releasing a billow of steam and white fluffy buns. Ma pictured a bowl of piping hot chicken noodle soup—a dish from back home he sorely missed.

Mee soup! Ma thought.

That's it! I will make mee!

Back in his shack, Ma mixed
flour, eggs, and water into dough.

He pushed and pulled the
dough, kneading again and
again, adding a bit more water
or flour until it felt just as it did
when he made it back home.

He rolled it.

He stretched it.

He looped it into long strands of mee.

Next, he cooked the chicken
and chopped it with a cleaver.

Out leaked its juice.

He tasted it. *Too dry!* he thought.

He shredded its meat with
his fingers.

A few minutes later:
Still too dry!

He snip-snap-snipped the meat with a pair
of extra-sharp kitchen shears and left it.

After an hour, he tasted the snipped-up chicken.

Yes, perfect!

With chopsticks in one hand, he pulled the mee noodles up high, unfurling long, golden strands. With the kitchen shears in another, he snipped the mee and twirled it into a bowl.

He topped it with snipped-up chicken. And finally, he ladled in the ingredient that made his mee like no other on the streets—a slosh of steaming stock.

Ma took a slurp. It was nourishing. It was comforting. It was a meal in a bowl.

Ng Shih came to mind, but he focused on the task at hand.

With no money to pay for a shop, Ma had to sell his mee on foot, lugging his wares around town.

Into a large metal bucket, he packed the mee, the chicken, the bowls, and utensils.

Into another, he packed the simmering stock over a stove of glowing embers.

He lifted the two buckets and seesawed with every step. *Whew! Too heavy!*

Ma found a pingga, a bamboo pole. He slung the buckets from both ends of the pingga and hoisted it onto his left shoulder. The load felt lighter!

He strapped his kitchen shears onto his apron.

CLINK,
    CLANK,
        CLINK!

The shears jangled as he plodded through the streets with his pingga.

After sunrise, Ma would trudge as far as his legs could carry him under the scorching heat. Just before sunset, he waited at the foot of a bridge for a flood of hungry students to surge by. He sang and performed magic tricks to attract passersby.

Everyone, rich or poor, could buy Ma's noodles. He made sure of that. A few centavos bought shorter snips. More centavos bought longer snips.

As customers slurped down their mee, Ma regaled them with stories of his motherland.

When he returned home late in the evening, he kicked
off his tire-soled shoes and slumped into a chair.

"Aiyo!" he moaned, rubbing his aching shoulder and
putting up his blistered feet.

Ng Shih came to mind, but he
focused on the task at hand.

Every night,
Ma made his mee.

Every day, he hobbled along roadsides and alleyways.

CLINK, CLANK, CLINK!

Soon Ma, with his pingga and shears, became known throughout Chinatown.
He named his soup mami: "Ma" after his name and "mi" for noodles.

CLINK, CLANK, CLINK!

"Mami!" customers shouted.

SNIP, SNAP, SNIP!

The day came when Ma didn't have to hawk his mee on foot.
He found a tiny space that fit two tables and a few diners.
Eventually, his noodle stall grew into a restaurant.

Yet, at night, Ma could still be seen on the streets in search of new customers. He'd knock on doors, giving away brown bags filled with steamed siopao buns or siomai dumplings from his restaurant. He also handed out cards that could be redeemed for free bowls of mami.

He gave away food to hospital staff and patients,

to flood and fire victims,

and to prisoners and public servants too.

Over the Christmas holidays,
Ma fed poor people in his restaurant for free.

The more he gave, the more he received, as word of his good deeds and good food spread across the city. People from port workers to the Philippine president became frequent customers and close friends. Ma's restaurant was the place where rich and poor people, unlike oil and water, mixed.

Inspired by Ma's success, imitations of his mami appeared all over town. To set his apart from the knockoffs, Ma's mee was nicknamed Mami King.

His business grew. And yet Ng Shih came to mind.

Ma sailed back to Canton.

His cheeks glistened with happy tears when he found
Ng Shih, the love of his life, still waiting for him.

This time, her parents
didn't stand in their
way. Because Ma and
Ng Shih showed them.
Their love for each other
was their fortune.

One day, a steamer carrying Ma and his bride chugged into the harbor of their new hometown. Ma beamed. He had created a place where everyone—rich or poor—could share their love for a bowl of mami. Indeed, he was Mami King.

Author's Note

This book is drawn from the information that's available about the life of Ma Mon Luk and bits I've gathered from one of Ma's living relatives, his grandson Francisco. Ma Mon Luk lived from 1896 to 1961 and didn't document all the details of his life story. While the major events of the book are true, I used my imagination to fill in the gaps. Consequently, the dialogue, Ma Mon Luk's thoughts, and some of the scenes in the story are fictional.

My mother, a Filipino, and my father, a Chinese immigrant who I didn't get a chance to know, met each other in Manila's Chinatown, the place where most of this story took place. I grew up in the Philippines. I've eaten mami. I've heard of Ma Mon Luk, the restaurant (my parents had eaten there before I was born). But I didn't get to know Ma Mon Luk's story until 2018. At that time, I was living in Norway and my book, *The New Filipino Kitchen*, which gathered stories and recipes of people of Filipino heritage from around the world, including the executive chef of the White House, was about to launch. An executive producer of a Netflix documentary series reached out and wanted to chat about street vendors in the Philippines and their backstories. While preparing for this meeting, I stumbled across Ma Mon Luk's story. I was completely spellbound! To me, it had the makings of a classic animated movie.

Writing this story myself never crossed my mind—not even in my wildest dreams—until 2020. Seeing this first picture book biography of Ma Mon Luk comes pretty close to my dream of watching Ma's tale on the big screen.

Illustrator's Note

I grew up in Baltimore, Maryland, as the daughter of Filipino immigrants. I had never read a children's book set in the Philippines, so I was thrilled when I was asked to illustrate *Mami King*. I shared the news with my mom, asking her if she'd heard of Ma Mon Luk.

"Wow!! Ma Mon Luk?!!" she responded. Her excitement took me by surprise, and she went on to say that it had been her and my father's favorite restaurant. "It was so good we could have eaten there for every meal, including merienda [snack]!" she told me. "We never got tired of it." My mom is an exceptional cook, so this was high praise. Then she said, "We were at Ma Mon Luk when your papa and I decided that we should marry."

Kristin Sorra's parents on their honeymoon in Baguio City, Philippines

How serendipitous! I had never known that my parents had been at Ma Mon Luk's restaurant when they got engaged, and I felt an even more personal connection to the story after learning that. I was more committed than ever to making every detail count and every page as beautiful as possible. In fact, I couldn't resist incorporating my parents into the full-spread restaurant scene near the end of the book, sipping from their bowls of mami.

Years ago, when my parents returned to visit Manila, they were sad to see that their favorite Ma Mon Luk restaurant branch was no longer there. I am grateful to have been given this rare opportunity to honor and immortalize their love story through my illustrations and Ma Mon Luk's story.

More about Ma and His Mami

Ma Mon Luk was born in 1896 in Zhongshan, Guangdong, in China. (At the time, the city and province were known as Xiangshan, Canton.) Due to poverty, Ma dropped out of school after junior high. He continued educating himself and was eventually able to get a job as a schoolteacher. Unfortunately, teaching didn't pay well, and Ng Shih's parents refused his proposal to marry their daughter. Ma left for the Philippines in 1918. This was after the fall of the Qing dynasty, the country's last imperial dynasty—a difficult time in China when hunger and poverty were worsening in the country.

Before Ma arrived in the Philippines, mee, or Chinese-style noodle dishes, were already common there. They were seen as food for poor folks. The most common was a stir-fried noodle dish called pansit. It is Ma, however, who is credited with inventing the recipe that made noodle soup, specifically Chinese-inspired egg noodle soup, appeal to the Filipino taste. He made mami (Ma's mee), a household name in the Philippines. Before Ma named his noodles "mami," the dish was called "gupit," a Filipino word meaning "cut with scissors." He cut the noodles according to how much his customers were willing to pay or could afford. Ma also cut chicken with sharp scissors instead of a knife—his self-proclaimed secret to keeping the meat juicy. Soon after he began peddling his mami, Ma gained loyal customers. One of them offered him a space just big enough to hold two tables and a few diners. The appetite for mami spread among the rich and poor alike. Ma's food joint grew into several restaurants, bringing people from different generations and walks of life together.

Ma died in 1961 at the age of sixty-five. His wife, Ng Shih, outlived him by twenty years. Ma and Ng Shih had three sons and a daughter, and after Ma's death, their sons took over the restaurants. They expanded the business to six branches, and two of those branches are still open today.

Mami has become a big part of Filipino food culture. Although Ma is famous for mami, he is also remembered by many for his generosity and kindheartedness.

Ma Mon Luk's portrait still hangs on the wall of one of his restaurants.

A modern-day Ma Mon Luk restaurant in Manila

About the People of the Philippines and the Oldest Chinatown

The people from the Philippines are called Filipinos. The ancestors of most Filipinos are the Native inhabitants of Southeast Asia. Because the Philippines was ruled by Spain from the 1500s to the 1800s, and by the United States from 1898 to 1946, some Filipinos also have Spanish and American ancestors. Trade with the Chinese people and their migration to the Philippines from as far back as the 900s has also led to many Filipinos of Chinese descent. Ma Mon Luk's road to riches took place in a district in Manila called Binondo, also known as the city's Chinatown. Formed in 1594 as a settlement for Chinese immigrants, it is the oldest Chinatown in the world. It was established by the ruling Spaniards at that time to keep a close eye on the growing Chinese population on the islands. Chinese immigrants were not allowed to own land and the odds of them getting a job were low, so most of them worked for themselves as vendors, traders, and business owners. In modern times, Chinese Filipinos own many of the largest companies in the country.

About the Carrying Stick and the Kitchen Shears

A pingga, or carrying pole, and a pair of shears have something in common. Both are simple machines. These devices help people get work done more easily. Both use levers and fulcrums. In the case of the pingga, the bamboo stick is the lever and the shoulder propping up the stick is its fulcrum. In the case of the shears, the levers are the blades, the fulcrum is the point where the blades cross. As you might have figured, levers are long objects, while fulcrums are points where levers pivot. The object you are lifting or cutting is called the load, and the force you apply to the load through the lever is called the effort. Levers help lift, move, break, or cut loads using lesser effort by multiplying the force you apply.

Bibliography

Sta. Maria, Felice Prudente. *The Governor-General's Kitchen: Philippine Culinary Vignettes and Period Recipes, 1521–1935.* Pasig City, Philippines: Anvil, 2006, 147–148.

Suryadinata, Leo. *Southeast Asian Personalities of Chinese Descent: A Biographical Dictionary.* Singapore: Chinese Heritage Center, Institute of Southeast Asian Studies, 2012, 736–738.

Torres, Jose Victor Z. *The Camino Real to Freedom and Other Notes on Philippine History and Culture.* Manila: UST, 2016, 7–13.

Ventura, Sylvia Mendez. *A Literary Journey with Gilda Cordero-Fernando.* Diliman, Quezon City: University of the Philippines Press, 2005, 96–97.

Vergara, Maria Shellane. "Mami and Mamon Luk." Academia.edu. Accessed November 6, 2023. https://www.academia.edu/5371650/MAMI_AND_MAMON_LUK.

My Easy Homemade Mami Recipe

Preparation time: 45 minutes, plus 30 minutes dough resting time
Yield: 2 servings

Noodles

5 ounces (140 g) bread flour or all-purpose flour
   plus a bit more for adjusting and dusting
¼ teaspoon salt
1 medium-sized egg (room temperature)
5 teaspoons (1 tablespoon + 2 teaspoons) water

Soup

2 ounces (50 g) shredded, cooked chicken
   meat (optional)
1 bunch baby spinach (trimmed, washed,
   and drained)
2 tablespoons chopped scallions
2 teaspoons sesame oil
20 ounces (600 ml) chicken stock (simmering)

Make the Noodles

1. In a big bowl, add flour and salt. Mix together with a fork.

2. Crack the egg into a small bowl. Add the water, and whisk with the fork. Pour into the flour and salt mixture, and stir with the fork until well combined.

3. Grab a handful of the mixture with your hand. Squeeze tightly and release. The dough should fall off your hand completely. (If not, add a tablespoon more of flour to the mixture. Blend well with your hand. Repeat step 3.)

4. Keep squeezing the mixture together in the bowl for about 5 minutes or until it all becomes one big dough. Form into a ball, and wrap tightly with plastic wrap. Let dough rest for 30 minutes.

5. Unwrap the dough, and lay it on a clean flat surface. Knead (push, fold, push, fold) the dough with your hand until the dough is completely smooth, about 10 minutes. Flatten and form into a squarish shape.

6. Sprinkle the dough lightly with flour. Spread flour all over the surface of the dough with your hand.

7. Using a rolling pin, roll the dough out into a large squarish-shaped sheet with sides of at least 10 inches (25 cm) long. (This requires at least 10 minutes of muscle power!)

8. Sprinkle the dough lightly with flour on each side, and spread the flour evenly with your hand.

9. Fold half of the dough over the other half without pressing. Sprinkle lightly with flour. Fold over again in half without pressing. Sprinkle again lightly with flour.

10. Find an adult to work with you. Ask the adult to slice the dough crosswise (across the folds) into extremely thin (about 2 mm) strips using a sharp knife. Sprinkle the cut noodles with flour, and toss to loosen the noodles. (Optional: Unfurl each strand, and stretch gently without breaking.)

11. Bring water to a boil in a big pot. Drop the noodles in boiling water and stir. Cook for 2 minutes. Drain.

Make the Chicken Noodle Soup

1. Divide mami noodles into two bowls.

2. Top with chicken (if using), spinach, scallions, and sesame oil.

3. Ask an adult to ladle the simmering chicken stock into the two bowls. Serve hot. ENJOY!

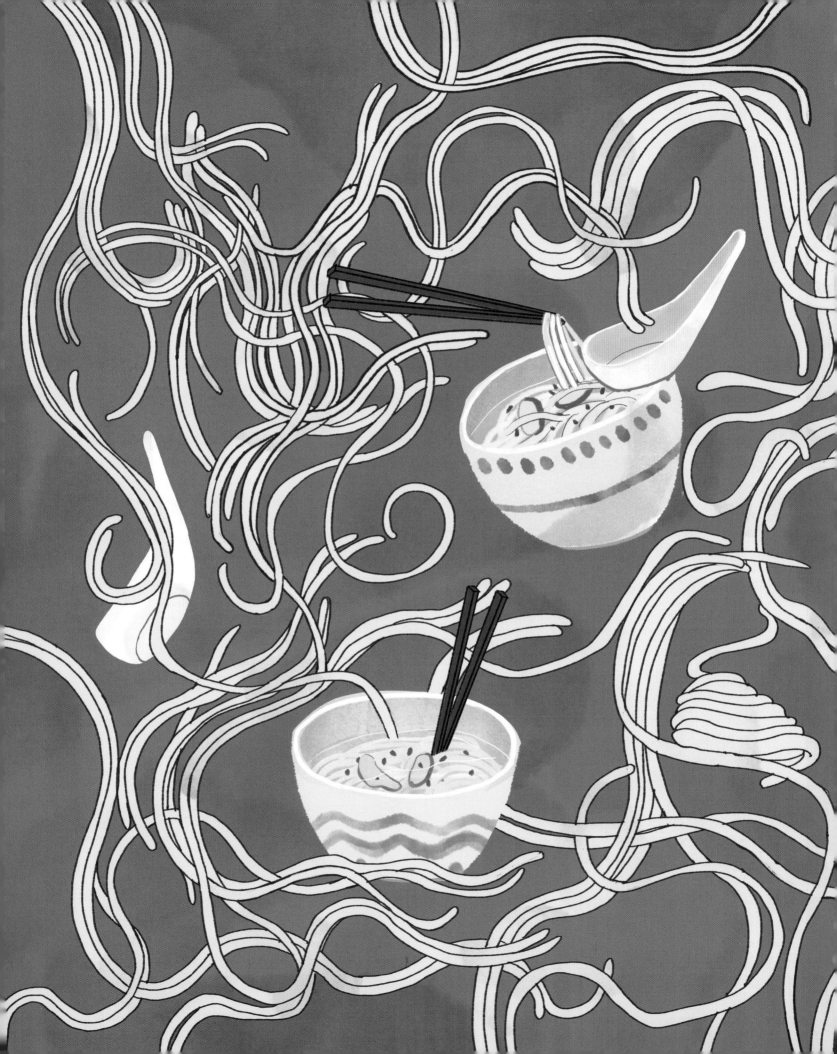